Human Nature and Political Systems

The Morning Notes of Adelbert Ames, Jr. (editor)
Soviet Leaders and Mastery over Man
Reflections on the Human Venture (with Charles H. Bumstead)
The Politics of Despair
How Nations See Each Other (with William Buchanan)
Public Opinion 1935–1946 (editor)
The "Why" of Man's Experience
Tensions that Cause Wars (editor)
Understanding Man's Social Behavior
The Psychology of Ego-Involvements (with M. Sherif)
Gauging Public Opinion (contributing editor)
The Psychology of Social Movements
The Invasion from Mars
The Psychology of Radio (with G. W. Allport)

Human Nature
and Political Systems

by Hadley Cantril

RUTGERS UNIVERSITY PRESS
NEW BRUNSWICK, NEW JERSEY

FOR TAD

The 1961 Brown and Haley Lectures are the ninth of a series that has been given annually at the University of Puget Sound, Tacoma, Washington, by a scholar distinguished for his work in Social Studies or the Humanities. The purpose of these lectures is to present original analyses of some intellectual problems confronting the present age.

Preface

The turbulence of our times is basically a turbulence in the human spirit. The situation men and women find themselves in today is, of course, a recurrent one in human history. They are seeking as they have sought for centuries the opportunity to live in peace with one another, to have a chance to get the satisfactions out of living that make living worthwhile according to the common consensus of people everywhere. But the situation now has a new sense of urgency because of the unprecedented frustrations and dangers created by unprecedented opportunities and hopes inherent in man's new artifacts and his new interdependence. What is required today, just as it was required at other critical times in history, is a self-conscious awareness of this human situation so the turbulence can be somewhat calmed and its component forces better controlled.

The profound and widespread changes which science and technology have brought about are proceeding with breakneck speed, like gales of wind which appear unlikely to let up and whose courses seem unpredictable.

New anxieties have been created by new uncertainties. Unprecedented choices are required. New frustrations are created as the revolution in man's aspirations goes ahead at an accelerating pace. Among people everywhere there is a growing awareness of the potential satisfactions to be derived from the miracles of science. So people are in a hurry, impatient to have standards of living raised and opportunities broadened. In many lands, there is widespread dissatisfaction with the means being used to achieve the goals expressed in brave and noble words by leaders on all sides.

Many values and standards are disappearing that once held groups of individuals together. People feel they are losing their sense of direction as familiar compasses prove poor guides under the influence of new forces.

Just what these forces are most of us only vaguely understand and just what their ultimate destination is no one knows.

While people may realize intellectually that they are living on a tiny and insignificant planet in a tiny and insignificant solar system, still that's where they are, that's where they have their being. In the grand scheme of the cosmos, problems that face Americans now such as integration, world wars, the emergence of new nations, the fall of other nations, the development and fate of democracy as a political experiment, are only fractions of a second in evolutionary time. But this is our matrix, these are the problems about which Americans must make choices and take action. These are our concerns.

In these essays I am trying to bracket and isolate what seem to me some of the major psychological aspects of the problems involved. I have a deep conviction that psychology has a responsibility not only to understand human behavior but to do what it can to increase the effectivity and quality of human living.

The particular level of abstractions I shall use in this accounting might be classified as falling in the field of "political psychology." It is to be hoped that it may be of some value to the political scientist more concerned with the formal aspects of political organization and change as well as to the psychologist more concerned with individual behavior. And I should also like to hope that this inquiry in political psychology might be of some use to those entrusted with the responsibilities of government.

These essays were written as the annual Brown and Haley Lectures given at the University of Puget Sound in April, 1961. I am grateful to President R. Franklin Thompson and Professor Lyle S. Shelmidine of that university for the opportunity and for their hospitality.

HADLEY CANTRIL

April, 1961
Princeton, New Jersey

Contents

1

Some Political Consequences of Being Human:

The psychological requirements
of political systems

In the book of Genesis we are told: "And God saw that the wickedness of man was great in the earth, and that every imagination of the thoughts of his heart was only evil continually. And it repented the Lord that he had made man on the earth, and it grieved him at his heart. And the Lord said, I will destroy man whom I have created from the face of the earth; both man, and beast, and the creeping thing, and the fowls of the air; for it repenteth me that I have made them."

3

Whether or not a person shares this view of God's creatures, the sample of man on earth is the only one we have and we must somehow put up with it. If mankind ran itself only by tropisms, instincts, or reflexes, affairs would certainly have a much neater and more certain order. But, of course, our lives would be lacking in all the subtle qualities that characterize human experience.

Not only is man endowed with a host of capacities which differentiate him from other species, but it would appear that certain basic aspirations have emerged and been filtered through the long course of evolution. As far as man is concerned, he seems not only pushed by the determined of the past but also pulled by the undetermined of the future as he tries to have his share in fashioning a better environment for himself. Living seems to be largely the attempt of an organism to create conditions within which it can carry out its purposes. Its direction is both *from* and *to*.

In describing this process, it is somewhat misleading to say that man is attempting to conquer nature. Instead, I believe he is trying to humanize nature by differentiating out of the total environment around him those aspects that appear to have

4

some potential significance to him and are seen as being useful, including the satisfaction that comes from having more comprehensive scientific or philosophical abstractions. Only if human significance is put into the equation can anyone trying to understand human behavior come out with any meaningful constancy, any repeatability, any form, any ordered change, any kind of value. It may be, of course, that science and the increasing scientific-mindedness of future generations will so de-humanize the environment that living may lose a good deal of its wonder and its warmth. If the moon comes to be regarded chiefly as a target for missiles or some day the destination for a week-end trip, it will no longer be the subject for romantic song.

Since human beings obviously cannot be satisfied by just *any* set of circumstances and since they are their own judges of the criteria that seem to make living worthwhile, some of the functional constants laid down in the human design by what biologists call the "code script" of our genetic structure should be noted here at the start. All of these characteristics assume different forms of expression and direction as they are nurtured and

5

channeled by the particular situations in which a person becomes enmeshed.

These requirements of human nature impose certain conditions on any political system that is to be viable. If it does not meet these requirements within the limits of man's tolerance, it will be snuffed out. So far no political system seems to have evolved and operated to meet all human requirements perfectly. And perhaps none ever will. Yet there does seem to have been progress, often sporadic, in the drama of human history toward political systems that better accommodate man's requirements and allow for development and change.

All aspects of human nature are intertwined and interdependent. But it is essential to differentiate them in order to describe them. Here are some to consider relative to man's political behavior.

One thinks first of all of such basic needs as those for food, shelter, and reproduction. Living the way Americans do, it is hard for them to imagine the urgency which the satisfaction of these needs has for millions of people who are still, literally, deep in the struggle for survival. Like many others who have traveled in Asia and Africa, I have seen people starving to death or slowly dying because of vitamin deficiencies in their meager diet. Unless and until such basic primitive needs are satisfied, people are interested in little else. Studies made by our research group show, for example, that among some of the poorest people in black Africa who have long been subjugated by the white man, the problem of racial discrimination itself has scarcely emerged in their consciousness, so desperate are they to find enough for their families to eat that day and the day after. Hence for such people concepts such as the "nation" or "national independence" are remote indeed.

Another requirement is that of security and stability—an adequate guarantee and protection of satisfactions so far acquired at whatever level. As we in the West tend to strive for more than we have we may tend to forget that for many people life is largely occupied with the protection of gains already made against threats that may come from nature or from other people. Francis Bacon observed long ago that "It is a miserable state of mind to have few things to desire and many things to fear."

If man's needs remained on the simple primitive level of food, shelter, and reproduction, he would obviously not be the very different creature he is from everything else on earth. What seems to me one of the human being's outstanding characteristics, developed somewhere along the evolutionary road, is his capacity and desire to experience value-satisfactions—satisfactions that encompass a wide range, variety, and complex of subtle feelings best described by the poet or conveyed by the musician and the artist in their particular mediums. This search for value-satisfactions leads to the diversity of cultural forms, to the refinements human beings create for themselves in satisfying such direct needs as food and shelter, and requires of any political system the possibility of experiencing these subtle overtones of feeling if living is to mean more than mere existence.

A sense of what these first three requirements add up to in a single individual is conveyed from part of an interview with a French tool- and diemaker who was asked a few years ago by a research colleague why he voted for the Communists. "I have to work under any system. I have my family to think of. The kids need shoes and the wife needs a coat. Where can I get the money? What the workers want is a good standard of living and more opportunities for themselves and their kids. I don't care if the workers get a good standard of living under capitalism or socialism. It doesn't make any difference to me. I don't want a revolution; I just want change. It's none of my business what workers do in other countries. They don't concern themselves about me; why should I concern myself about them? Let them fight their own battles and I'll fight mine. But nothing I say is going to make any difference. All I want is to enjoy myself in this life. For all I know it may be the only one I have. When you're dead, maybe that ends it. I don't know. All I want is to have a good life, that's all. Is that too much?"

And closely associated with man's capacity to experience what I call value-satisfactions is an attribute that seems to me the most characteristically and uniquely human of all: the desire to experience new and emergent value-satisfactions. Both the course of individual development and of history seem to show that it is characteristic of man never to be satisfied, always to be somewhat discontent no matter how high his standard of living, no matter how great his opportunities, no matter how distinguished his accomplishments. No one who is plugged into reality seems able to maintain a completely complacent, neutral world where his aspirations are neatly balanced by his achievements. As soon as a person becomes aware of some new *potential* satisfaction, he apparently wants to experience it for himself. And sometimes people pursue these new potential satisfactions in spite of the great cost and the uncertainty to which they may lead.

This ceaseless human striving has, of course, been the theme of much of man's accomplishments. Dostoevski describes how man apparently quite knowingly and with full comprehension puts aside his advantages "in favor of some other plan, and betakes himself to a road, to risks, to the unknown, to which no agent or agency has compelled him, as though, unwilling to follow the appointed path, he preferred to essay a difficult and awkward road along which he must feel his way in darkness. . . . Man is essentially a constructive animal —an animal forever destined to strive towards a goal, and to apply himself to the pursuit of engineering, in the shape of ceaseless attempts to build a road which shall lead him to an unknown destination." [1]

The attainment of such value-satisfactions and increasing satisfactions is possible for man alone because of those characteristics he has which are more frequently emphasized but which, in spite of their obvious importance, seem to me essentially instrumental in their functions: such capacities as high intelligence and reasoning, the ability to form abstractions, the ability to imagine what might be, and the ingenuity to devise ways and means of making what is potential become more proximate and real. An eminent neurologist, Sir Russell Brain, has stated that for human beings "symbolization is an inherent function of the nervous system" and along with man's capacity to have feelings and emotions, it developed, like his distance receptors, as an instrument for maintaining purposes through time. [2]

Any list of human characteristics must include the fact of individual differences in capacities, abilities, and sensitivities. I remember once when I was a young instructor at Harvard the difficulty a candidate for the doctor's degree had in answering questions put to him during an oral examination by various members of the examining committee. In the discussion of whether or not the candidate should sustain the examination, Professor Whitehead asked for the floor saying he wanted to make a few remarks about the nature of "intelligence." He likened each person's intelligence to a mountain range with its many peaks and valleys and its own unique contour. Having worked with this young man closely for three years, Professor Whitehead went on to describe his particular peaks and assured us that by some statistical fluke our questions had hit him in his valleys. The candidate was passed.

And so it is with all of man's wide-ranging characteristics. When someone once pointed out to the Negro composer and singer, Huddie Ledbetter, the contrast between the way he and another man sang a certain blues song, Leadbelly replied, "But he's he and I'm me." Individual differences become of the utmost importance in considering the difficulties likely to be encountered by societies which contemptuously disregard those differences or try to smooth out each man's peaks and valleys, forcing everyone into a few standardized patterns for the sake of efficiency or political conformity.

So far this rough listing of some of man's characteristics begins to show that political systems must provide not only secure and ever improving standards of living but also secure and ever developing standards of quality, standards of excellence, standards of value that can serve as reference points by means of which an individual steers his own living in a direction he will sense as progress.

These characteristics can be transformed into still other dimensions and requirements the human design imposes on any political system. So the listing continues, essentially slicing the same pie in a different way.

Every human being wants to create some sort of real identity and integrity for himself. This is clearly seen in the effort of growing children for self-expression with all its ramifications for the process of socialization. Once some identity has been achieved, then the struggle continues to maintain it or to enlarge and improve it according to the cultural pattern at hand. The process

13

is exemplified by the lack of morale experienced by people in industry or in an army if for long periods of time their jobs are standardized to a fixed routine. A play by the great Czech dramatist, Karel Capek, gave the word "robot" increased currency in our vocabulary, a word Webster defines as "one of a large number of artificially manufactured persons, mechanically efficient, but devoid of sensibility." We can turn again to the perceptive Dostoevski for a description of what we mean: "Even if man *were* the keyboard of a piano, and could be convinced that the laws of nature and of mathematics had made him so, he would still decline to change. On the contrary, he would once more, out of sheer ingratitude, attempt the perpetration of something which would enable him to insist upon himself; and if he could not effect this, he would then proceed to introduce chaos and disruption into everything, and to devise enormities of all kinds, for the sole purpose, as before, of asserting his personality. . . . Every human act arises out of the circumstance that man is forever striving to prove to his own satisfaction that he is a man and not an organ-handle."[3]

Closely associated with the need for identity is

man's need for meaning, not necessarily highly intellectualized but at least a feeling that his own existence, his own living makes sense. Unless this sense of meaning is satisfied, the human being is so constituted that he becomes bored or seeks some escape, possibly in drink, sensual pleasure, deviant behavior, rebellion, or sheer work. The existentialists have brought this problem to the fore in Western thinking. Nietzsche pointed out that "he who has a *why* to live for can bear almost any *how*."

A slightly different way of saying almost, but not quite, the same thing is to say that every human being also craves a sense of worthwhileness, a feeling of self-respect rooted in a faith in his own values and a confirmation of their reality in his own behavior, sometimes quite irrespective of what others may think. This sense of worthwhileness is the feeling every person has of wanting to be wanted and needed, to be appreciated. A satisfying relationship to the universe is apparently unobtainable unless an individual feels he is playing a role in it. Martin Buber has described this as man's "instinct to make everything into *Thou*, to give relation to the universe, the instinct which completes out of its own richness the living effective action when a mere copy or symbol of it is given in what is over against him."⁴ People want to be respected for what they are. For example, an Italian farmer whom we interviewed in the course of our research some years ago said, "I feel that I just don't count as a person. No one cares one way or the other what happens to me or to my family. We drift along from day to day. All the officials care about is what we can do for them and seeing that they get their taxes. The Church wants its share. Yet what do we get out of it all? Who cares about us?"

From the psychological point of view, many of the characteristics of human beings that are labeled as "needs," stem fundamentally from a person's desire to experience the consequences of his own purposive actions based on his own decisions. Stated somewhat differently, it means that the human being gets much of his satisfaction from the effect he sees his behavior has on other people; satisfactions that come from the feedback a person experiences from others. Everyone experiences his identity and his sense of worthwhileness chiefly from the reactions of other people to what he does.

All of this is, of course, related to and indispensable to an understanding of the concept of "freedom" which is basically a psychological, rather than a political, concept. "Freedom" if it is to be meaningful at all must be connected to some self-started action that brings about some desired results. This means, incidentally, that what one person regards as freedom is not necessarily freedom for someone else. One man's freedom is another man's bondage. Different people require different types and qualities of freedom according to their levels of development, their levels of social and political maturity. If an undisciplined, undeveloped people—like a young child—are given complete freedom, chaos and disillusionment are likely to result since they will not be in a position to recognize their own best interests, and, even if they do, will not know how to go about pursuing them. If men are to enjoy the blessings of freedom, they must learn through experience to build up a set of constancies, a pattern of assumptions, which will produce a reality world within which flow can proceed from form. Otherwise chaos or anarchy result. The great British scholar, Lord Acton, felt that the one most sure and sig-

17

nificant thread running through the course of man's history was to be found in his search and fight for freedom. Albert Camus has called freedom "the only imperishable value of history."

What are the psychological functions political systems serve and why do political systems exist in any form? These questions can only be answered if human society is viewed as a self-creation with separate individuals forming themselves into a people as part of their ceaseless attempt to fashion an environment within which their human characteristics may be gratified, nourished, and perfected.

It appears that any small group quickly discovers that specialization and cooperation enable it to satisfy its individual basic needs more efficiently. And since human beings are not endowed with elaborate instincts which guide so many forms of life to fixed patterns of marvelously organized social behavior, men must create their own organizations, make their own rules and regulations, and either find their own leaders or live under the sufferance of someone or some group who gains power. These are required if interdependence is to guarantee that different jobs will get done, that the rewards of joint effort will be distributed, that production and distribution can be counted on, that individual responsibilities are learned and met, and that the gains made are protected.

The first organic communities on the planet seem to have arisen in Mesopotamia after man had invented and developed agriculture to such an extent that he could give up his nomadic existence. These village communities with their primitive democracy are apparently among the oldest political units on earth. Their first public building was a temple where goods were stored and distributed and where the first written records known to us consisted of accounts of the daily transactions that went on under the supervision of the high priest. The leaders in man's earliest political systems seem to have been temporary kings or rulers elected for special emergencies, such as war, and whose offices disappeared when the emergency was over, although some of these individuals were not slow to find reasons for making their positions more permanent and fashioning a society with different classes.

Poets and novelists have described how every

individual is an island unto himself and how in one way or another we are all continually trying to reduce the loneliness, sometimes filled with an awful anxiety, that accompanies this inevitable solitude of individuality. To do this people must gain a sense of stability in the midst of the impersonal forces that surround them. They must impose an order on disorder to get a repeatability of satisfactions they can count on. They want support. They want both physical and psychological security.

People can achieve this security if along with others in their community they collectively create and follow certain norms that set limits to segments of behavior for their mutual benefit. The Cross Cultural Index begun years ago by Yale anthropologists lists dozens of customs and patterns of belief and behavior that seem to have arisen in every single society known, past or present: kinship regulations, rules for trade and exchange, status systems, labor regulations, marriage and burial rites, property rights, penal systems, etc. While many of these do not necessarily require political systems for their continuation or enforcement—for example, hospitality rites

—in nearly all instances the proper exercise of these functions becomes a concern of organized government.

But there is far more than security and a relief from our separatenesses as individuals to be gained by social grouping. There can be no conception of "self" apart from a conception of "others." And no one can recognize a consistent pattern of behavior in others except for the constancy of "self" which he develops, with all its assumptions, purposes, and values, and which he brings to every occasion.

A person learns very early in life that the quality of his relationships with others is vastly enhanced if he takes into account the way *they* experience the same events that *he* is experiencing. This simultaneous awareness of the significance of his own experience and the probable significance others are experiencing provides important links in the psychological chains that bind people together, and adds new dimensions to life.

As noted earlier, the source of many of man's characteristics such as his need for meaning, for identity, or for worthwhileness, come fundamentally from his desire to have the satisfaction of experiencing intended consequences from his own behavior. And it is of the utmost importance in understanding social and political life to remember that for most human beings everywhere the ultimate criterion for judging the effectivity and consequence of behavior is in terms of the reaction other people show to it, either directly or indirectly.

Everyone knows the rich satisfaction that comes to him when through some act on his part he is able to make the experience of others valueful. The most cherished experience the human being can have and the "highest" he is capable of we describe by the word "love." Love, if it is to have any meaning at all, is the feeling that comes only when the satisfaction another person derives from his own experience is a necessary requirement for the satisfaction to be derived from our own experience. Love is therefore completely unselfish. As Juliet said to Romeo, "The more I give to thee, the more I have."

Indeed, it is the sharing of significances that makes any situation or event "social." From the psychological point of view culture itself can be defined as a fixed pattern of common significances. Experimental investigations show that a person can learn the inadequacy of his assumptions in a relatively painless way if he shares the assumptions and purposes of others whom he is observing and with whom he has an empathic relationship. By seeing the mistakes and difficulties the false assumptions of other people may lead to, one can quickly learn to revise his own assumptions.

The building and maintenance of a political system enables this sharing of experiences to proceed under some fixed though changing form and to insure that goals can be translated into concrete action. For example, in discussing the important role played by the Communist Party in Cuba, a perceptive reporter has pointed out that "the (Communist) Party needs Dr. Castro and he needs the Party and their relationship is cemented by this fact. Ideology requires organization to survive and there is no Castro organization in this sense." [5]

The compounding of shared experiences into a bundle furthermore means that an image characterizing a political system can be projected; an image that serves to focus thought or allegiance and that may be viewed by others with apprehension, curiosity, or wonder. This was nicely illustrated in an account of the conversations and spec-

23

ulations on a ship bringing a number of elderly
Italians to begin life anew in America. In reporting
what he overheard among these people, a jour-
nalist wrote,

> . . . And the word that turned up most frequently
> in their conversation was "America". In colloquial
> Italian, "America" has come to mean something more
> than a geographical place. It is, by extension, any
> deposit of hopes, any tabernacle where all things too
> big, too difficult, too far beyond one's grasp take
> shape and become true—so true that all one needs in
> order to touch them is a ship that will take one there.
> "America" is, again, something one finds or makes, a
> stepping stone, a rung in the ladder that allows one
> to climb a little higher—not, of course, in the coun-
> try called America but back home. "America" also
> means the treasure one finds when "America" (the
> rung in the ladder) is steadily under one's feet. Inevi-
> tably, the question that the old people asked one
> another, over and over, was "Is America *America*?" [6]

As an individual's participation with others dem-
onstrates its usefulness and as its consequences
become registered as part of his reality world, he
builds up loyalties and allegiances. The loyalties
of each one of us vary to some extent in their roots,

their intensity, and their range. When the original satisfaction they brought because of their utility ceases to confirm assumptions or enrich values, then loyalties become formalized and empty or are given up altogether.

The concept of "nationalism" and loyalty to a "nation" hardly exist at all among many people in undeveloped areas of Asia, Africa, or Latin America. It takes time before people whose loyalties have been bounded for centuries by a tribe, a village, or a community can experience the consequences of "national" action in their own living. One of the great psychological advantages of the city-state, such as Athens, was apparently that it was small enough to be understood as a focus for identification and still powerful enough to enhance an individual's sense of his own strength.

Programs now being carried out by the government of India to improve conditions in Indian villages have shown that these projects, by and large, are successful only if the villagers themselves have a voice in what is to be done, are encouraged to take some initiative and hence feel some responsibility. By following such simple common-sense principles, not only do retaining walls get built and wells get dug, but a new respect and loyalty is engendered for the larger political unit which has helped to make all this possible.

Loyalties are formed and preserved only when an individual senses the strength they bring and recognizes the source of this strength. The great contribution of Karl Marx was his renewed emphasis on the value and dignity of work with all the wide-ranging loyalties this created when workers became organized into political units under skillful leadership. This is illustrated by a conversation with a young engineer in Leningrad when I was there in 1958:

Under Capitalism, Russia was weak, was under the influence of other nations, was economically poor, and a third- or fourth-rate power. Under Socialism, Russia has become a great power and the great majority of people here attribute their own greater well-being and, above all, the increased prestige of Russia in the world to Socialism. Despite the terror and bloodshed by which all of this was achieved, the terror and bloodshed take second place to the achievement itself. World War II was a mathematical proof of the soundness of the Socialist system for Russia. Only a few unimportant people oppose Socialism and they do so for special selfish reasons that are not shared by the overwhelming majority in the country. It follows that when a foreigner insults Socialism (Communism), it is equivalent in the minds of the Soviet people to insulting Russia as a nation and therefore the Russian people.

Political systems not only enable an individual to extend himself in space by acquiring national or regional loyalties but they also enable him to extend himself in time. By articulating and handing on the memories of those who lived in the past and who shared similar loyalties and by holding up a vision of what lies ahead, the present takes on added significance and hope. For many people in the world today, living has a dismal sameness and routine that blots out any concern with what past generations have done and gives no incentive to plan for or think about the future. For this reason, men who lead a people into new nationhood are quick to embody the past into a set of myths and to paint a picture of a glorious tomorrow. In the creation of the modern state of Israel it is apparent how important a piece of land has become as a symbol of identity by means of which the past could be dramatized and the future made more secure.

Human beings could not build up the self-constancies they do nor maintain their wide-ranging identities and loyalties unless there were some way to hang on to them, to recall them at will, to give significance to immediate behavior in the here and now by relating it to more universal values not so bounded by time and space. Man accomplishes this feat through his capacity to create symbols, beliefs, images, and myths. He becomes the "time-binding" organism Korzybski has called him. A psychological function of symbols is to hold reality worlds together by giving a person something to cling to, aspire to, hope for, or have faith in. They extend his reach and enrich his dreams, enabling him to define and envision goals. The devout Muslim who kneels several times a day to pray always facing Mecca is reminded of the spiritual bonds that link him with millions of his brothers no matter how isolated he may be physically.

Beliefs are in part outgrowths of the fact that all human perception is basically a probability, a bet we make that things and people and situations are what we think they are, that there is correspondence between what is "out there" in the world and what we assume is "out there." But since no one can act effectively in his everyday life by self-consciously analyzing the nature of the probability facing him, he transforms these probabilities into certainties and absolutes.

This characteristic of man means that it is in his very nature to believe. It allays anxiety; it brings comfort; it makes social life what it is. It extends the loyalties and significances he can take into account far beyond his own immediate concrete experience by making institutions, nations, and ideologies real for him. By preserving, fostering, or creating symbols, myths, and beliefs and by devising rituals such as rallies, oaths, national anthems, salutes to the flag, or prayers, political systems enable people to identify themselves with larger values and to experience in their own lives what these values refer to. And there seems to be a tendency for each political form to lay down principles and precepts which it assumes are universal for all mankind.

An example of the way in which a symbol serves as a sponge to soak up a wide variety of meanings may be seen in the currency of the symbol "Fidelismo" in Latin America. As a *New York Times* reporter has written: " 'Fidelismo' ranges from plots for implanting Castro-type regimes to simple sympathies for the Cuban social experiment. It is shot through with extreme opportunism, with extreme left-wing politics and with the extreme idealism of starry-eyed youth. It is confused and combined with pressures for land reform, general social protest, Latin American solidarity, rabid nationalism, anti-Yankeeism and revulsion for 'imperialism' and 'colonialism'. . . . 'Fidelismo' is more a state of mind than a political movement." As the reporter indicates, such a symbol is bound to appeal to the millions of people in Latin America who have been "condemned for centuries to virtually sub-human misery." [7]

The world is now full of examples of nations trying to achieve status, trying to maintain or enhance their national egos. For example, some small nations that can hardly afford to do so maintain travel bureaus and have a few jet planes; others for similar purposes of prestige maintain bombing fleets or try to develop their own atomic bombs; the Indonesian government is building a great stadium and a large hotel for the 1962 Asian Games even though its people are economically desperate with one of the lowest per capita incomes in the world.

As men have been told ever since philosophy was born, these symbols and beliefs easily turn into stereotypes and prejudices and can become substitutes for thought and for a growth in sensitivity. A friend of mine once overheard a conversation in New Orleans in which one man said to another, "It ain't what folks don't know that makes 'em so damned ignorant, it's the things they know that ain't so." And, of course, people hang on to these stereotyped beliefs until they are so frustrated by them that they simply have to change their assumptions in order to carry out their purposes. There is a story of a New England farmer who was owed one hundred dollars by a neighbor for many years. At long last the neighbor came to pay his debt but was told, "I'd rather not take your money so I won't have to change my opinion of you."

The same concept also, of course, is often perceived very differently by different people. For example, the great American citizen, Ralph Bunche, is regarded in the United States as a Negro and his son was refused admission to a tennis club because of that. But in some countries of tropical Africa, Mr. Bunche is not regarded as a Negro since he is not really black.

In the course of man's history and in the modern world today it appears that human beings are able to live (although with very different qualities of living) in a wide variety of political systems ranging from almost complete slavery to almost complete freedom. In terms of a longer perspective, every political system can be regarded as both an achievement and an experiment just as can every individual life.

The nature of the experiment depends, of course, upon the circumstances of the time including the level of political maturity of the people, the extent to which they are threatened by nature or by their neighbors, and the natural and human resources available. The American historian, F. J. Turner, is remembered for his thesis that "Not the constitution, but free land, and an abundance of natural resources open to a fit people, made the democratic type of society in America for three centuries." [8]

At present in many parts of the world the most

diverse and incompatible forces are being brought to bear on people who are trying to work out modern political systems of their own. In describing the political problems of present-day Morocco, an observing correspondent wrote:

> In the bazaars that rim the mountainous Berber regions one can today visit apothecary stalls and purchase medicaments popularly used: talisman verses of the Koran, wrapped in gilt paper; dried lizards, weasels and hedgehog quills, to burn away the vapors; mandrake roots and asphodel bulbs.
>
> Not many miles from these rude pharmaceutical displays are lined up long rows of American fighter planes capable of traveling at twice the speed of sound and H-bombers.
>
> The clash between ultramodern and antediluvian makes for a troubled political atmosphere.[9]

Whatever form a political experiment takes, one can make a choice of resigning himself to the temper of the times or of insulating himself as much as possible from the ways of the world. But neither of these relatively easy courses will satisfy a person who wants to be and to become his independent self within the framework of the potentials available in his social and political environment.

2

The Quality of
Political Awareness:

Psychological development and inertia

There seems to be something in human nature that wants out, that wants to be released and revealed, that wants to become aware of itself, that wants to be preserved. This spirit of man is the ultimate source of political organization and of political change whether orderly or violent. It is the hub around which political systems revolve for all the divergent groups who come to share a national ideal and nationhood itself as man devises, no matter how imperfectly, ways and means to enhance his self-esteem and nurture his self-development. So far no political system yet achieved seems to have taken completely into account the multitudinous aspects of human nature—some gross, some wondrously subtle.

Those skilled innovators of statecraft, this nation's founding fathers, in emphasizing man's unalienable rights, sought to guard against the consequences of his unbridled passions by placing their faith in the rational side of human nature. But years later, a great political scientist, Graham Wallas, was to point out: "Whoever sets himself to base his political thinking on a re-examination of the working of human nature must begin by trying to overcome his own tendency to exaggerate the intellectuality of mankind."

On the other hand, some systems tend to treat man as an object, assuming his nature can be hammered into almost any shape, and demand his unconditional surrender to the state. In his well-known little book, *The Greek View of Life,* G. Lowes Dickinson has written that "Aristotle, for instance, declares that no one must suppose he belongs to himself, but rather that all alike belong to the state; and Plato, in the construction of his ideal republic, is thinking much less of the happiness of the individual citizens, than of the symmetry and beauty of the whole as it might appear to a disinterested observer from without." [1]

What are some of the psychological requirements for political organization? What is the psychological matrix within which political forms arise, flourish, or fade away? In trying to answer these questions, it would be senseless to construct a model of man. Man must be dealt with as he is found to be. Albert Camus has noted that if any conception of an abstract man is preferred to a man of flesh and blood, then existence is denied as many times as necessary and resentment must take the place of love.[2]

Before delineating some of the psychological conditions under which political development goes on, the enormous variety of situations in which people of the world now live should again be recalled. It is not a simple matter for a person to get a real feeling of situations that differ from his own unless he has an opportunity to be an active participant in them. For full-bodied human situations involve on-going stresses and strains, aspirations and disappointments, hopes and anxieties, con-

39

flicts and overlappings of purposes. Unless behavior is described by a particularly gifted writer who is also a perceptive observer and himself immersed in the social matrix he is writing about, the subtle nuances and interplay of social interactions are lost. All too often the observations of social scientists are those of an outsider looking in with the result that much of the data gathered, though of great value, must still remain a somewhat scratchy playback of the improvised symphony social life is with its many overtones and its interwoven major and minor themes. It is the same difficulty anyone has in knowing what another person is "really" experiencing, especially if that person is quite unlike us in background and temperament.

Let me try to describe as an example an experience I had a few years ago in India. I had been invited by a psychologist to spend a few days at his university to lecture. The university was in a town of approximately 400,000 people. My friend told me ahead of time that there was no hotel in town and the only place for visitors, nearly all of whom were Indians, consisted of a large cement area with a crude covering where people could sleep. Since his own home was modest and crowded he had thoughtfully made arrangements for me to stay in what he said was one of the two best houses in town. This was occupied by a young American, his wife, and their children. It had become a source of much recent comment because air conditioners and an electric refrigerator had been installed by the American agency under whose auspices this truly dedicated young man was trying to help villagers improve their farming techniques.

When I arrived at the house I was shown into the huge guest room with its cement floor and walls and a single lamp suspended from the high ceiling. In one corner was a bed with a straw mattress on a rope frame and a mosquito netting over it. There were two small windows in the room without glass but with bars characteristic of an American jail. My adjoining private bath had a cold water spigot up on the wall and no other equipment whatever. There was not a hook or nail on which to hang clothes, and I was told by my hostess to be sure to keep everything locked in my luggage during my stay.

As I became acquainted with the situation I learned some of the worries facing this young mother trying to run a household and bring up her three children in a distant land but, still, as I said, in one of the two best houses in town. She had seven servants, several of whom were bearers spending much of their time running around town delivering or collecting messages since there was no telephone. Other servants had to keep close to the children whenever they went outside to protect them from poisonous snakes. As is so characteristic, nearly every servant had brought his large family, including uncles, aunts, and cousins, to live in the back yard of the house which was a source of supply. The mistress of the house had to keep the key to the icebox in her pocket and open and close it herself when meals were to be prepared. Nothing could ward off the flies or mosquitoes that swarmed in the open windows. People seemed to be milling around everywhere. No motion picture or tape recorder could ever convey the true psychological atmosphere of this microcosm. It was little wonder to me that the young woman wept when I got on my plane some days later to return to America. For she still faced several years of living in a situation which was at best difficult for an American used to her own ways of doing things. On the other hand, the native Indians seemed extremely happy and cheerful living in this comparative security and luxury.

If one visits an Egyptian village with its water buffalo walking around in circles to propel the Archimedean screw still used to lift water from the canal to irrigate the fields in the neighborhood, with its row on row of small and flimsy dwellings, with the high mud walls surrounding the more pretentious houses in town, with its small mosque and its simple and unrelieved daily routines, one begins to see how small are the worlds in which people live. These villagers, like most Indian villagers, know little else than what they have become used to and do not really comprehend that their fate could be much better than it is. The drama of their lives is found in small occurrences such as an illness, a new romance, a new baby. Everyone wants more children even though people cannot take care of the children they already have, for children are an Egyptian farmer's riches and the larger the number, the higher the status of the village wife. The boundaries of the village are the boundaries of the world for its inhabitants, and most of them have little curiosity about what goes on beyond these boundaries. Yet here, as in India, one

43

feels that these lovable people are also fairly happy and not weighted down with trouble. They laugh readily.

It is not only among the so-called underdeveloped people that the world is circumscribed with individuals having a self-centered interest in their own affairs. In our own country, for example, where people are charged with the responsibility of having a sufficiently informed opinion so they can govern themselves, there are great areas of ignorance that must be associated with lack of concern. Through a national survey, I recently found that among the approximately 100,000,000 adults in the United States, 50 million of them do not know who Nehru is; 79 million do not know what the initialed abbreviation, AEC, stands for; 50 million cannot correctly identify Charles de Gaulle; 20 million think Russia is a member of NATO, while another 20 million just don't know one way or another. But 85 million do know about Marilyn Monroe and 80 million can identify Mickey Mantle.

I mention these instances only to bring out the point that people will not alter a political system themselves or even be ready for improvements and revisions in what they have, let alone in more drastic political revolutions, unless they are somehow psychologically ready.

What does it mean to say that people are "ready" for something else?

Clearly, no people living under wretched conditions and hampered by illiteracy and ignorance are going to be concerned with much of anything except the immediate satisfaction of their needs and specific reforms that might bring this about if they feel there is a chance of success. General Kassem who came to power after the revolution in Iraq continually points out that before his people can decide on what long range form of political system they want, they "must at least be self-confident, and they must at least not be hungry."[3] Aldous Huxley has noted that unless human beings are "given a fair chance" they can never be expected to pass abruptly from a primitive state where they may have been ruled by a despot to a successful state of self-government.[4] In view of all the technological, economic, demographic, and organizational problems involved in creating modern political systems, stages of development cannot be completely skipped in the building of a political system any more than they can be skipped in the development of an infant into a mature adult. A psychiatrist, Dr. Bryant Wedge, has noted certain parallels between the development of a nation and the development of an individual. At a certain stage of its growth a nation will, for example, act like a newly emancipated adolescent, exhibit extreme self-consciousness and self-determination, and resent aid that is offered (and that perhaps must be accepted for survival) if it in any way emphasizes a feeling of dependence. Political maturity, on the other hand, involves a frank recognition of a people's own best interests and a willingness to accept as well as to give without loss of self-respect.

The psychological problem to be resolved by economic, technological, or political aid is a problem of speeding the transition through the various stages required so that people *can* have the "fair chance" to become self-consciously aware of the sort of political system they would like to achieve. During the struggle of the Indonesians to free themselves from the Dutch, public conveyances in the streets of the large cities had printed on them in English, "All men are created free and equal." But a recent observer in Indonesia has noted how the people in that turbulent land, who a few years ago were quite willing to bear their frustrations because of the blessings they thought freedom was going to bring them, now regard freedom only as an amusing slogan because of all the frustration and corruption to which an abrupt passage to freedom has led.[5]

Before any political development can occur, there must not only be a sense of the inadequacy of the present situation but an ability to assess it in terms of new goals which take on a certain new reality because some means seem available to accomplish them. Frustration, if it is to be creative, must involve a sense of the inadequacies of both objectives and practices together with a sense of the possibility of transforming something potential into something real. Before the "bloody Sunday" in 1905 when the Czar had his soldiers fire on petitioners who had come to urge him to take action that would relieve their misery, our own Mark Twain had expressed his hope that the Russian people would somehow discover "the high road to emancipation from an insane and intolerable slavery." [6]

It is important to stress the obvious point that

it is not enough merely to realize the gap between one's own world and the dream of what might be. The dream must have in it some workable way of making itself come true. Sometimes the way in which a sensed frustration can be realized is more a feeling than a reasoned judgment. In fact, it would appear in the course of history that it is just these vague feelings that something *must* be done that lead to the devising of ways to show how something *can* be done. For example, in speaking of the American colonies and their reaction to the Stamp Act of 1765, a historian notes that "much of their reasoning was inexact, but their feelings were clear and sharp." [7] From then on the colonies gradually devised effective means of linking potential action to their own real world of existence, thereby making that existence itself a base for directed effort and achieving a new political unit which was not too large to enable them to maintain an identification with it.

It must always be remembered that economic, technological, and political developments involve people—and people must learn to perceive the relationships of new facts, new machines and medicines, new ways of organizing and doing things to their own purposive strivings. Otherwise, these developments will never become part of a people's reality world, a part of them.

So in a very real sense people must learn what they *do* want. They can't possibly know what they want until they are aware of what is available, of what is potential. They are like many young Americans in late adolescence who can't figure out what they want to "be," what they want to "do" in life, and who have as yet only a vague idea of the range of possibilities open to them.

The so-called underdeveloped people want "civilization" and "progress," but often they are not at all clear as to what these concepts might or should stand for and refer to concretely. They must learn. Otherwise they will accept cheap substitutes and be led up blind alleys. The business of telling people what they should want is the great opportunity of totalitarian dictators just as it is the great opportunity of democratic communities. In this situation, the Soviet and Chinese Communists have a certain subtle advantage over more advanced countries since they, too, are coming up from a relatively recent undeveloped state and it is easier for them to project themselves into the minds of more backward people than it is for Americans with their fabulously high standard of wants.

Without underemphasizing in any way the much discussed revolution of aspirations going on in the world, there are still many millions of people who do not really seem to expect changes to take place in the foreseeable future. They have not yet learned what their aspirations can be. But their new leaders, among others, are trying to tell them.

It also seems that people must learn the sad truth that once they know what to want in terms of a better society and a more effective political system, they must work and organize if they are to realize these wants. A major problem in Pakistan is to convince people of the reality of the old saying that they must learn to help themselves and that this struggle is often long and hard. One of the greatest concerns of the government in New Delhi is to show people what work is and to teach them that it is only through work that the income of themselves and the country can be increased and standards of living raised. Many poor Brahmins who have no more than an acre of land will nearly starve to death rather than till the land themselves. As one of my Indian friends put it, "In India, people work like kings and live like slaves, while in your country, people work like slaves and live like kings." This same friend, a college president, called a special meeting of his several thousand students to have me describe how American undergraduates work at part time and summer jobs to help pay for their education. Many Indian villagers keep waiting for the "government" to send someone to make simple improvements which they could easily have made themselves with a little cooperation and a willingness to cut across caste and social lines.

As pointed out earlier, some of the attributes of man, such as his feeling of self-confidence, become experientially real only when he sees there is a good chance of taking appropriate and effective steps to achieve his goals. In considering political development, this interdependence of purposes and a surety in the sequential significances of behavior that will carry out these purposes must be constantly borne in mind. People easily become either apathetic toward or anxious about the ultimate goals they would like to achieve through political organization if they continually sense a lack of reliability in means to accomplish these goals. This is true, for example, with respect to the yearning of men and women everywhere for lasting peace.

Furthermore, and most important, political development will not proceed unless an individual actually experiences some desirable consequences, some confirmation of the effectivity of the steps taken to achieve his goals. He must sense that the new participations he has become involved in and the new responsibilities he has assumed in one way or another do lead to new satisfactions. The point was expressed by an Italian worker who was interviewed some years ago in a study of voting behavior:

> The workers are by now quite indifferent to politics. They don't take them seriously any more because they have so often been disappointed and disillusioned by political leaders who talk big but who don't carry through. The workers seem to be turning away from political parties. They see no use in them.

Certainly one of the prime reasons for the rise of strong leaders in some of the nations of Africa, Asia, or Latin America is due to the fact that earlier parliamentary regimes had dismally failed to keep up with the growing political consciousness of the people and had not guided it into desirable channels. Hence, the whole idea of parliamentary government became discredited as a façade for the selfish rule of a small governing class. There has been tragedy in the Belgian Congo because the people there were so completely unprepared to take proper advantage of the independence they so deeply desired and so wildly celebrated when it came. After eighty-four years of Belgian administration, still only about half the people in the Congo could read and write, there were only sixteen Congolese university or college graduates and not a single Negro doctor, engineer, or lawyer among the population of nearly fourteen million people.

If political changes are to last, it appears that they must ring true and have some moral basis. In spite of the great shortcomings of Athenian democracy with all its restrictions concerning sex, race, and color and with its slavery, its great moral contribution was that it did introduce for the first time into the world the idea of individual freedom and individual responsibility within a civic organization.

53

Washington stated that "morality is a necessary spring of popular government." And only recently Tom Mboya, the dynamic leader of Kenya, said, "It is the compromise with principle to accommodate colonialism and racism practiced by countries in the West that undermines the moral capacity of the free world." [8]

Political development in an interdependent world further involves the problem of finding identifications that enlarge one's sense of worth-whileness and importance. Especially in nations that are just beginning to come into their own is there a groping for broader identifications that will be meaningful in terms of a particular culture and body of traditions and a particular stage of development so far reached. The Muslim religion is spreading rapidly in Africa as an effective replacement of narrow tribal religions; identification with Islam, not hampered by being a white man's religion, provides a sense of new importance, of membership in a much larger community and a pride in belonging to a more modern world.

In discussing the reaction of the colonies after the Boston Tea Party, Carl Van Doren points out that "for the first time in their history the scat-

tered colonies were united in a common senti-
ment . . . sympathetic toward Boston, the colonies were apprehensive for themselves . . . the
common feeling among the colonies led to a common action." [9] In his study of *The American Mind,*
Henry Steele Commager describes how the American environment with its mixture of national
groups, its spaciousness, and its mobility, gave rise
to hundreds of different organizations in "an effort to give an appearance of stability to an unsta-
ble society, to create order out of disorder, to sub-
stitute new loyalties for those which had been
dissipated and new conventions for those which
had been lost, to enlarge horizons and inflate opportunities." [10]

And in advanced societies today, the fantastic
development of science and technology and the
increasing role played by the state in personal life
seem definitely to have created what the British
philosopher, John Macmurray, has called "the crisis of the personal." People are having increasing
difficulties squaring what they know with what
they believe and what they believe with what
they know. As religion tends to decline, the state
tends to be regarded more as an apotheosis with

55

the consequent danger that "the sense of personal dignity as well as of personal unworthiness will atrophy" and "ideals of sanctity or holiness will begin to seem incomprehensible or even comical. Success will tend to become the criterion of rightness, and there will spread through society a temper which is extraverted, pragmatic and merely objective, for which all problems are soluble by better organization . . . the state is then compelled to perform the functions of the church (for which by its nature it is radically unfitted) and its efforts to do so will produce, the more rapidly the more whole-hearted they are, a crisis of the personal." [11] This warning takes on particular meaning if we remember that many people are coming into a state of nationhood when technological and industrial possibilities are far different from what they were at the time of our own Constitutional Convention. Hence, the problems of nationhood are exacerbated and the potentialities enlarged. As various people have pointed out, it is part of the irony and tragedy of our times that so many new nations are coming into being just as more and more sophisticated observers of the human scene are realizing how invalid the idea of self-sufficient nationhood is. The point was well expressed by Stuart Chase.

> On balance it is certainly a gain to have the new nations out from under the yoke of colonialism. One wonders however how they can function as sovereign states, touchy about rights and real estate, and at the same time be serviceable members of that world community which the age demands. Their leaders cannot play lead soldiers indefinitely. Their budgets cannot long tolerate the dead waste of a large military establishment. This holds for the Great Powers too, but is more acute among the new members of the United Nations. A formula is badly needed which can combine local pride and autonomy with planetary co-operation, and it must apply to all the nations of the world, great and small.[12]

In addition to the obvious craving for a higher standard of living that pushes many people today to more adequate political systems, there are basic psychological forces also goading them on: their sense of inferiority relative to the West, their sense of humiliation because of their backwardness and because they have been so long kept down. Just as these psychological forces are important in understanding underdeveloped nations, they are

57

equally important in understanding the enormous progress made by the Soviet Union whose people for centuries realized that their nation was a third-rate power and that their pace of development was far outstripped by progress in the West. These factors lie behind the great idealism of some modern political leaders as well as the idealism of youth in many lands. In one of our group's investigations, for example, we found that over half the university students in India, whom we asked to tell us about their personal aspirations, indicated that they wanted to lead a life of service to their people and to their nation. Incidentally, this aspiration was mentioned by less than 20 per cent of a sample of American undergraduates.

People living within nations that have "arrived" and fulfilled many of their goals often find it most difficult to understand the motivation of those who are still on the march, still going through earlier stages of development. It is important that we become sensitive to the new patterns of what may constitute status and prestige that will doubtless emerge in countries where political and social institutions are in a state of flux as, for example, in Ceylon or Afghanistan. Furthermore, we even tend unwittingly to place ourselves at the geographical center of the world in our use of such terms as "Middle East" or "Far East." The government at New Delhi, for example, uses much more objective descriptions such as "West Asia" or "East Asia."

The primary criterion by means of which a political system is tested is that it provide sufficient political stability for the realization of individual needs and for directed, purposeful change to achieve ever greater human satisfactions. It is a continuous creation. This requires an organization that can become the repository and the symbol of the values and aspirations of the people, as well as one that can provide for, or allow the development of, effective instruments and mechanisms to give those values concrete reference in the daily lives of its citizens. When the gap between what is supposed to be and what is becomes too great, a political vacuum is invariably created that is bound to be filled in one way or another. In such critical situations we expect new norms and new social patterns to emerge. We witnessed the emergence of new political organizations in the Workers' Councils that sprang up spontaneously in the early days of the Hungarian Revolt in October, 1956, and assumed many of the functions of government before they were blotted out by the second armed Soviet intervention in November.

Political stability that provides both form and flow, of course, requires trained and dedicated leadership. Furthermore, leadership even in relatively stable societies must be creative. Jacques Maritain has observed that "everything begins in the spirit, and all the great events of modern history have been formed in the inmost soul of a few men." [13] Effective leadership in a democratic society requires such ingredients as the ability to formulate over-all goals which can serve as guides for proposals and actions; a talent for effectively communicating goals; the ability to devise means for achieving goals; the capacity of resourcefulness in meeting new and changing situations; the ability to provide people with a sense of participation in the process of government; the ability to see with the eyes of the people and to feel with the hearts of the people; the foresight to help people in his country, no matter how "advanced" it may be, learn what they should want for a good life.

In many non-Western areas of the world where

individuals have had no chance to achieve political maturity, where social change is spotty, sporadic, and uneven, the leaders who emerge, if they are to remain leaders, must wield their power and guide their people in wide-ranging activities, including under the cloak of political development many aspects of personal and social behavior which we in a more mature, democratic West would regard as an infringement of personal rights. In describing the new state of Ghana, an observer has written that it "is authoritarian and the authority is Mr. Nkrumah. He has followed the classic modern pattern—the creation of a personally controlled party that reaches into every village and directs every aspect of social and political life . . . Mr. Nkrumah has as his base a country he shaped himself and that greets him with love and laughter almost everywhere he goes." [14]

In the message Benjamin Franklin prepared for the Constitutional Convention indicating why he would vote for ratification, he wrote, ". . . I agree to this Constitution with all its faults, if they are such, because I think a general Government necessary for us and there is no form of Government but what may be a blessing to the people if well administered, and believe further that this is likely to be well administered for a course of years, and can only end in Despotism, as other forms have done before it, when the people have become so corrupted as to need despotic Government, being incapable of any other." [15] Tyrannical dictators gain power, Albert Camus has observed, when they are able to "secularize the philosophies that give them the right to do so." [16] In maintaining the state and themselves at the head of the state, they create political mechanisms all too likely to subordinate with their efficiency the aspects of human life that make living worthwhile. "In all the world's higher religions, salvation and enlightenment are for individuals. The Kingdom of Heaven is within the mind of the person, not within the collective mindlessness of a crowd." [17]

Sometimes certain people become impatient with their fellow men, including their fellow citizens, when political systems are not remedied or changed quickly. In focusing on the potentialities of man's nature many people sometimes forget its limitations. Then they lack the compassion necessary for understanding. While a person may completely agree with Lester Ward that "government is one of these artificial products of man's devising, and his right to change it is the same as his right to create it," he may lose sight of the fact that there are many obstacles, some of them psychological, to be overcome before man is ready to exercise his right to change.

What are some of these psychological obstacles?

For one thing, the sheer state of desperation some people are in with respect to the satisfaction of their needs and the gain of some personal security makes it almost impossible for them to take the first steps necessary for development. They are afraid to give up what has "worked" for generations, sometimes for centuries. They feel that the acceptance of anything new is too great a risk to take, that experimentation is madness. No matter how little people are able to take for granted, they generally become aware of what they are taking for granted only when it is threatened. The sole guide to the present comes from the past. A fable from Southeast Asia describes the situation:

Once there was a frog which could walk like a man. Determined to go on a journey into dangerous unknown territory, he plodded along by the usual jumps from all fours. At times, however, to survey the terrain ahead, he reared up on his hind legs and for a while went forward like a human. In this position, his eyes were looking backward, but of this limitation he was unaware. Consequently, the frog felt reassured. Wasn't what lay in front familiar? And wasn't it accustomed, comforting and safe? Ignorant of the real perils into which he was heading, the frog went on, judging a new situation by the one from which he had come.[18]

There is much more involved in this than ignorance. There are compelling, urgent, immediate situations that must be met. For example, in a study of a sample of very primitive South African Bantus, our research showed that because of the overwhelming worry these natives had that they would not have anything to eat the next day, they feared that either they or their children would have to steal, take to crime, or commit murder in order to survive at all. While such desperation often leads to rebellion, it cannot lead to directed and planned change or to revolution unless, as I have repeatedly stressed, a person can bet on or experience more satisfying consequences under new conditions. The Egyptian fellah "fights change because it is not proved to him that a change is good for him. He fights it also, because he is ignorant, superstitious, suspicious. It is a vicious circle. The conditions in which he lives invite and nurture disease. The disease that wrecks his body saps his strength and his initiative." [19] Egyptian social scientists estimate that about 85 per cent of the population live on this hand-to-mouth level.

Another roadblock is the frequent resistance to technological developments because of the sheer inertia of habit. For example, it is not easy for people who for centuries have roughly timed their activities by the sun or the seasons to see the need for the more precise measures of time required by modern agriculture, modern industry, and modern communications. A recent survey by the British Institute of Public Opinion revealed that about two-thirds of the English people over sixty-five years of age felt that all experimenting with rockets, satellites, and space travel should cease and human beings should stick to the earth.

Sometimes the improvements technological advances bring about are fundamentally so little understood that they are not accurately assessed. An illustration of the contrast in point of view between Westerners and Asians is shown from an experience I had in Madras. The convocation of the All-India Science Congress to which I had been invited took place in a specially constructed and beautifully decorated *pendal* (a tent arrangement but without sides) which seated about 5,000 people. During the ceremony, the foreign delegates took their seats on the platform a few minutes before Prime Minister Nehru and his official party of dignitaries were to arrive for the formal opening. Shortly before their arrival, the man in charge of platform arrangements noticed that the ice was unevenly distributed in the two pitchers of water beside Nehru's chair in the center of the platform. So he rolled up his sleeve, reached down in one pitcher, picked up some ice, put it in the other pitcher, and then stirred both pitchers with his hand.

Two days later there was a knock on my hotel room door and three medical doctors from the Indian Public Health Service said they would like to talk to me about a practical problem of motivation that was concerning them in their job of trying to get villagers to use latrines. They reported that villagers just saw no sense in the whole business

66

and, particularly, did not want to give up the use of the fields because they liked to be together and gossip in the warm sun while taking care of nature's needs. They complained of the loneliness of latrines. I cite this subsequent visit by the Public Health authorities for in illustrating to them the way I was beginning to understand the problem of hygiene and sanitation in India, I mentioned the incident of Nehru's water pitchers. They listened to me quietly, then turned and asked, "But what was the matter with that?" For them as for all of us, intellectual knowledge alone has little effect on the assumptions brought to an occasion. I would guess that very few of the sophisticated Indian scientists present at the convocation actually "saw" this behavior because the reality world they used to filter and guide their perceptions was so different from our own.

A third roadblock consists of certain beliefs and ideologies that have become so much a part of a person that he cannot give them up without a painful rending of himself. I was told by an agriculturist in the Near East that many older farmers in his area object to the use of insecticides because they feel it goes against the Koran. In India the combination of the hereditary caste system imposed centuries ago on the native inhabitants by their Aryan conquerors combined with the Hindu religion and its concept of reincarnation, produces a complacency, a lack of ambition, a disinterest in progress, and a consequent indifference to the fate of individuals which the great Gandhi spent his life trying to change. The practice of detachment of "the empirical self" from the "true eternal self" turns into a socially sanctioned escape from responsibility and the practiced renunciation of the goods of this world. The caste system permits an undemocratic disregard of the welfare and feelings of persons in lower castes who can be ordered about in gruff ways which no American worker would stand for, but which in India do not seem to concern anyone particularly since nothing else is expected.

Sir Julian Huxley points out that increasingly adequate visions of destiny require that "both the actualities and the possibilities of the external environment and of human nature" must be taken into account. "If knowledge is lacking on which to build a coherent and satisfying vision, imagination will almost universally be called on to provide mythical explanations and interpretative extrapolations of actuality; and these imaginative formulations may then canalize and condition the whole culture." [20] If the absolutes man creates in his belief systems are to prove useful for political change, they must be self-consciously regarded as man's own functional creations and not as God-given static abstractions.

A fourth roadblock to political development comes from the loyalties man acquires that give him such psychological security and enlarged identity. In a study of a small Italian community, Edward Banfield found that the general rule often guiding life was to "maximize the material, short-run advantages of the nuclear family." [21] As a result, no one was interested in the larger group or community unless he clearly saw it was to his personal advantage; no one concerned himself with public affairs for they were considered to be the job of paid officials; anyone who exhibited an interest in or dedication to the public welfare rather than to private interests was regarded as a fraud, etc. Daniel Lerner and his associates have shown how these narrow loyalties persist as long as people have little exposure to larger cultural units because of limited forms of communication of any kind.[22] Improvement and enlargement of political forms require alteration and variation in institutionalized forms of communication if the complexity and interdependence of man's relationships to man are to be properly illustrated, illuminated, and explained.[23] In view of the many restricted traditional loyalties that still bind so many people together, it is little wonder that these people remain relatively unconcerned about national problems or that international problems are quite outside their range of recognition; many such problems simply have no apparent direct personal relationship to life.

Finally, we should mention as another roadblock the great variety of institutions and governmental forms often perpetuated for one reason or another no matter how inadequate they may seem to be if one looks at them with any perspective. In a study of the political dynamics of the Philippines, Lloyd Free begins his report with the following paragraph:

> The American in the Philippines does not have to journey to the outlying province where head-hunters recently bagged six Christian heads in pursuance of

their courtship rituals to realize that he is in a culture decidedly more primitive than his own. All he need do is to enter the lobby of the imposing Legislative Building which houses the Philippine Congress in the modern city of Manila and read this sign:

HOUSE OF REPRESENTATIVES
INFORMATION
Firearm is prohibited inside Congress Building
Deposit firearms here

If he wants to understand the political facts of life in the Philippines, this should serve as an initial warning that, along with his firearms, he should deposit any preconceived standards he might have brought with him from mid-Twentieth Century America having to do with cultural mores and political practices and ethics.[24]

In some instances, if people sense that progress is going on in spite of the fact that they are not participants in the government, they feel no compulsion to have any voice themselves in the political process. An observer in Pakistan wrote that "even remote villagers have heard of or seen the sweeping land reform, the resettlement of tens of thousands of refugees from India, the stringent curbs on smuggling, black-marketing, hoarding, and bribery. That all this has been accomplished under martial law rather than democracy has made little difference to the average Pakistani." [25]

The autonomous and sovereign city-states which developed in classical Greece and made it quite impossible for any larger political unit to be peacefully formed seem to us today fantastically unrealistic. To the historian a thousand years from now our own conception of sovereign nation-states will doubtless seem just as fantastically unrealistic.

3

Pressures and Possibilities:

*The emergence and competition
of political systems*

In 1928 Carl Sandburg could write:

Now it's Uncle Sam sitting on top of the world.
Not so long ago it was John Bull and, earlier yet,
    Napoleon and the eagles of France told the world
    where to get off at.
Spain, Rome, Greece, Persia, their blunderbuss guns,
    their spears, catapults, ships, took their turn at
    leading the civilizations of the earth—
One by one they were bumped off, moved over, left

behind, taken for a ride; they died or they lost the
wallop they used to pack, not so good, not so good.
One by one they no longer sat on top of the world—
now the Young Stranger is Uncle Sam, is America
and the song goes, "The stars and stripes forever!"
even though "forever" is a long time.
Even though the oldest kings had their singers and
clowns calling, "Oh, king, you shall live forever." [1]

A few years later this same perceptive recorder
of the human venture described

. . . . man as a struggler amid illusions,
each man fated to answer for himself:
Which of the faiths and illusions of mankind
must I choose for my own sustaining light
to bring me beyond the present wilderness? [2]

As the gap between the rich and the poor becomes more and more noticeable to the poor, if
not to the rich, the poor will, of course, act as
quickly as they can to close it. In doing so they
must put their trust and faith in some political
system as the instrument to bring them beyond
their present wilderness. The speed with which
millions of people will become increasingly aware
of the quality and range of experiences human

beings are capable of, given a fair chance to achieve an advanced civilization, is bound to accelerate with modern means of communication. An Italian labor leader once remarked in an interview that "there is likely to be great danger when the hopeless begin to hope." The danger is, of course, that hopes may not be fulfilled as aspirations run far ahead of what it is humanly possible to accomplish even with the greatest effort and good will in the few years that constitute the foreseeable future for men and women who tend to project time from the vantage point of their own span of life.

It is especially important for us to become completely and continuously aware of the fact that non-Western societies are involved in what Lucian Pye has termed "multi-dimensional revolutions" with sweeping changes occurring simultaneously on a number of fronts rather than in the relatively ordered sequence they followed in the course of our own Western development.[3] In the laudable effort to increase the education of people at all levels there is in many countries already a critical problem of finding positions for individuals whose aspirations have gone up with their education and who find no place to go in their own country and hence are likely to become frustrated and bitter. In India I met several families where sons had completed graduate work in the United States, England, or France entirely at the expense of the Indian government but who could find no compatible position in India and had accepted excellent opportunities in Sweden or Canada. Sometimes situations change so quickly that what is becomes a travesty on what might be. After Saudi Arabia suddenly became wealthy with the exploitation of its oil resources, King Saud got a private plane and had it equipped with a revolving throne and a jukebox.

Americans must furthermore try to bear in mind that the newly developing nations—like our own fledgling country nearly 200 years ago—are *simultaneously* faced with two important problems: on the one hand, the problem of creating and building up an internal domestic economy and political system which will satisfy the needs of their people and, on the other hand, creating and projecting on the world scene an image of their nationhood which will command respect and insure their own national dignity and integrity.

When we in the West look at emerging political systems and try to foresee others yet to come, we quite naturally tend to use as our standard of reference the political patterns that now exist and to which the West has become accustomed. But new conditions and new situations produce new resolutions of political problems and if the standards of judgment used to understand and evaluate them are too restricted, then understanding and judgment can prove tragically misleading. Many people, for example, are now only vaguely aware of the importance of larger regional groupings of different nations in various parts of the world as a probable necessary step toward the creation of a truly united system of nations. A few years ago the independent Federation of Mali was formed uniting the two autonomous republics of Senegal and Sudan on the coast of West Africa. Nasser has recently created the United Arab Republic. Many other regional political groupings are in the offing.

Some perspective can be gained by a brief glance at a few of the different political systems emerging today, each of which seems to be something rather new under the sun.

China is a nation where over 600,000,000 people

are governed by an absolute dictator, Mao Tse-tung, who apparently has gained an even greater power than Stalin whom he so much admired. Mao and his leading associates, half of whom represent the military, have the conviction that "the central task and highest form of revolution is to seize political power by force, to solve problems by war." [4] Peace loving people were shocked by Mao's statement that he would willingly sacrifice half the population of China to win a third world war. Like some other dictators in history, he is apparently regarded by millions of people as a charismatic leader and seems to have convinced himself of his own infallibility and of the universality of what he holds to be the truth. The communes he established, designed to help Red China make its great leap, destroyed family life, blotted out privacy or chance for solitude, and took away opportunity for independent judgment. A student of modern China points out that Mao's formulations "bear little relation to reality, and then, given the authority with which his power endows them, it is reality that must be made to conform to the slogans." [5]

In Pakistan—a nation whose people are largely illiterate and who have had no experience in self-government—President Ayub Khan is drafting a constitution which aims to create small democracies in the form of village councils which, in turn, will elect a president and members of the national assembly. The promise is that when the councils have proved effective and people have achieved some political sophistication and sense of national responsibility, then national officials will be elected directly. In the meantime, a strong central government is held to be necessary to delegate what powers it feels are appropriate to the various provinces. In Indonesia, President Sukarno's highly publicized "guided democracy" or "democracy with leadership" has a parliamentary membership strongly representing functional groups such as labor, farmers, and the armed forces. This type of political system with a parliament composed of the parties within the nation and the functional groupings, somewhat in the patttern of a corporate state, obviously depends for its effectiveness on a leader whose popularity is widely rooted in the people.

One of the new leaders of Africa, Julius Nyerere, has pointed out how the emerging people of his continent need time to find their own ways of democratic government. He indicates how established

Western democracies may misinterpret the African search for democracy because of their assumption that democracy must involve a multi-party system. The political units emerging in Africa, he says, are not so much political parties as nationalist movements and "it would surely be ridiculous to expect the country—for the sake of conforming to a particular expression of democracy, which happens to be seen in terms of a government party and an opposition party, and mid-stream in a struggle that calls for the complete unity of all its people —voluntarily to divide itself in order to produce a ready-made Opposition at the moment of independence." [6]

The way in which a political organization serves not only as a social movement but as a whole way of life is dramatically symbolized by the statue of Nkrumah which stands in front of the Ghana House of Parliament and displays prominently on its base the inscription "Seek ye first the political kingdom and all others shall be added unto it." In some of the newly developing countries, the need of people for a national identity seems to be even stronger than the desire for a higher standard of living which is taken for granted once a national identification a person can be proud of is securely established. For Americans who achieved nationhood over 150 years ago and who have passed through so many stages of national development, the force and inclusiveness of nationalistic movements are likely to be lost sight of until the history of their own country is self-consciously reviewed. The list could be expanded almost indefinitely, so rapidly are old ties disappearing and more indigenous bonds beginning to link people together as they try to speed their development.

The statement issued by eighty-one Communist Party leaders in December of 1960 after their meeting in Moscow said that, "Our time . . . is a time of struggle between two social systems." [7] Like the poles of a magnet, each of these systems for one reason or another attracts some people into its field and each struggles to become a more dynamic center of influence with the word "center" defined by Webster as "a source from which a force, influence, process or the like, takes its origin."

The enormous strides the Soviet Union has taken in improving the standards of living of its people, in providing them security in life, and in giving them a pride in their country's accomplishments are impressive indeed. Masses of people in the uncommitted areas of the world watch with a mixture of anxiety, skepticism, and hope to see if the sort of democracy we have can be adapted to their needs and can successfully compete with monolithic, authoritarian governments which ironically call themselves "peoples' democracies." Looking at the situation from inside the Western world, a knowledgeable observer of the ideological struggle now going on, Sir Charles Snow, writes that "We (in the West) are becoming existential societies and we are living in the same world with future-directed societies. . . . We seem to be flexible, but we haven't any model of the future before us." [8] Millions of men and women everywhere are wondering if, in terms of their own interests and their own problems, our American democratic leadership will actually lead.

America has many assets: her geographical position, her natural resources, her industrial capacity and experience, her people, her wealth, her standard of living. But more important than all of these is the factor which makes America what she is and except for which America would not be America:

the factor the New England abolitionist, Theodore Parker, in 1850, labeled "the American Idea." At a meeting in Boston, Parker said, "There is what I call the American Idea. This Idea demands as the proximate organization thereof, a democracy—that is, a government of all the people, by all the people, for all the people: of course a government on the principle of eternal justice, the unchanging law of God; for shortness' sake I will call it the Idea of Freedom." [9]

This phrase of Parker's—"the American Idea"— describes something more than "an American vision" or "an American dream." The word "idea," says the dictionary, "can mean an embodiment of the essence of something." The American Idea has substance; a substance that has been created as men called "Americans" have confirmed their hopes through actions and thereby made vital, living, and real their faith in what America stands for. On the great seal of the United States, reproduced on our one dollar bills, is engraved the phrase *Novus Ordo Seclorum,* New Order of the Ages. Long ago the philosopher, Hegel, wrote that "America is the land of the future where, in the ages that lie before us, the burden of world history shall reveal itself." The kind of behavior, the ethical codes, the challenges, the aspirations, and the whole orchestration of experience the phrase "the American Idea" refers to has, of course, been indelibly set down by characteristically American writers such as Emerson, Whitman, Mark Twain, William James, Dos Passos, Steinbeck, and Robert Frost, among many, many others.

Just as the world had never before seen anything quite like the American Idea when it was first embodied in our Declaration of Independence, so the world never before saw anything quite like the Soviet Idea which became operationally effective at the time of the Bolshevik Revolution. As I have noted elsewhere,

> from Lenin on down, Soviet leaders have told man that he must and can create his own history by fashioning an environment that will provide an increasingly good life for workers. These leaders realized earlier that a Marxian utopia was not an inevitable development of history but one that could be achieved only by ceaseless struggle, guided by a highly controlled and closely knit organizational machine which had to destroy whatever stood in its way, including, not only capitalism, but any char-

acteristics of man likely to conflict with or weaken
the precise objectives of the state as defined by the
Communist Party . . . The idealized goals which
Soviet leaders have always held up to the "masses"
are goals which, they believe, can only be achieved
by following the one and only truly "scientific" ideology of Marxism-Leninism, an ideology it is the
right and duty of the Communist Party to interpret
according to the situation at hand.[10]

Just what these two competing ideas refer to can
be made somewhat more precise if we differentiate
and contrast the assumptions each one makes about
human nature and the function of political systems.

In the American Idea the overriding major prem-
ise and the basic assumption is that the individual
human being is the unit, the measure, the building
block. It is the individual human being who has
the needs, wants, intentions, hopes, and aspirations. It is the individual human being who does
the deciding, who makes the judgments, who initi-
ates action, who does the doing. And it is the individual human being who experiences the consequences of his action, who is satisfied, disappointed,
or surprised. In the Soviet Idea the all-important
unit is the State with individuals regarded essen-

tially as its servants and as productive units within it. The primary duty of every Soviet citizen is his obligation to the State which provides him security from cradle to grave and expects undeviating loyalty in return. Furthermore, the State itself is regarded as an instrument of the Communist Party to be organized and manipulated according to goals laid down by Party leaders. The Party is regarded as everlasting while the State is something to be used until it can wither away, even though all signs so far point in the opposite direction.

As a consequence, an integral part of these contrasting assumptions is in the American Idea the belief that man not only should participate in setting the goals of his own destiny and the way in which these goals are to be achieved, but that man has the capacity and competence to make such choices. In the Soviet Idea is the assumption that human beings are rather simple creatures who do not really know what is good for them or how to achieve what is good for them and who must, therefore, be completely directed and controlled by a select Party elite who are highly trained in the science of making the political decisions necessary for the welfare of the State.

These two assumptions combine to spell quite contrasting ways of looking at freedom. The American Idea stresses liberty and freedom for all, not simply for a few. And freedom, if it is to be meaningful, must be a freedom *for* as well as a freedom *from.* In the American Idea, freedom is for people of diverse backgrounds and diverse capacities to live on equal terms of respect with and for each other. It is freedom *to be* and freedom *to become.* It is freedom *to make good.* In the Soviet Idea, freedom is defined in the standard Soviet Dictionary as "the recognition of necessity." This means a person is free only insofar as he understands what the Party feels is necessary and right. Concepts such as "independence" and "initiative" in the Soviet Idea refer to "the display of the greatest self-denial and the readiness and ability to obey an order absolutely whatever the obstacles and dangers. . . . Initiative is a discipline not of simple obedience, but a discipline linked with the effort to obey the order, direction, or command received in the best possible way and, even more than that, linked with the readiness always to do your duty without waiting for an order or a reminder but showing 'initiative'." [11] Obviously Party goals cannot be realized if personal independence is tolerated. Hence individuals are both free and independent only when they have learned to be "self-guided" helpers of the State.

In the American Idea, the concept of responsibility is the opposite side of the coin of freedom. The founding fathers early recognized that freedom without responsibility leads only to anarchy while responsibility without freedom is slavery. The American Idea has conceived of freedom and responsibility in this interdependent relationship because of the assumption that man is, after all, responsible for his decisions, no matter how much they may be determined by the experiences of his past. Our law looks for the "intent" of a person accused of crime. In the Soviet Idea, the characteristics of man are to be manipulated by changes in his socioeconomic conditions and by massive, systematic, and continuous indoctrination so that responsibility turns into a learned self-discipline in which the sole criterion of responsible action is the welfare of the State.

An assumption of the American Idea is that any group of people has the right to organize itself and through a parliamentary government be in charge of the political system so long as public confidence is retained and so long as those parties or groups not in power are assured the right to be heard. Tom Paine called the freedom obtainable through representative government "the invention of the Modern World." The Soviet Idea, on the other hand, assumes that once the Communist Party has gained power, then every and any means are justified to maintain that power with no effective opposition of the people allowed to organize itself, and with the courts and the "elected representatives" of the people being further instruments of the self-perpetuating Party leadership. One of the theses enunciated by the Second Congress of the Comintern held in 1920 stated that "Every Communist member of parliament must bear in mind that he is not a legislator seeking agreement with other legislators, but a Party agitator sent into the enemy camp to execute Party decisions . . . (Communism) has a strong interest in having reconnaissance units in the parliamentary institutions of the bourgeoisie to facilitate the work of destruction." The recent tactics of Mr. Khrushchev in the United Nations, as well as the behavior of Soviet representatives in other world organizations, such as UNESCO, would seem to indicate that this precept is still taken seriously.

The American Idea as it operates today believes in open societies with the right of self-determination. Americans know that no people in the world have ever voted themselves into a Communist state, and they welcome coexistence. The Soviet Idea holds that "peaceful coexistence of countries with different social systems does not mean conciliation of the socialist and bourgeois ideologies. On the contrary, it implies intensification of the struggle of the working class, of all the Communist parties, for the triumph of socialist ideas." [12] The fate of such countries as Lithuania, Hungary, and Tibet shows that the Soviet Idea will not tolerate national independence.

The American Idea assumes implicitly the inextricable interweaving of means and ends and would completely agree with what Karl Marx himself once wrote: "An end that requires unjust means is not a just end." Incidentally, I suspect that if Marx could again walk the earth, he would be much more favorably impressesd by what he found in the United States than in the Soviet Union. He would probably gaze with incredulous astonishment at the huge portraits of himself which hang from time to time in Red Square, in a nation where no labor unions are permitted and where the State has zealously taken over and retained most property, although the ultimate goal Marx envisioned was that man should transcend the very notion of property and there should be no such thing.[13] The Soviet Idea assumes that the objectives laid down by the Party elite justify any means for their attainment. One of Lenin's most familiar precepts is that a good Communist must be ready to "resort to all kinds of tricks and ruses, to employ illegal measures, secretiveness and concealment of truth" whenever necessary.[14] This tactic is in operation in many different ways today, including the use of attractive symbols such as the statement of the Communist leaders who met in Moscow that the aim of Communism is to create "independent national democracies."

Finally, the American Idea with its conception of the dignity of man recognizes the complexity of human nature with its capacity and desire for

93

choice and participation and for the experiencing of individual patterns of values and affections. "There is no democracy among human values, however each may cry out for an equal vote," said Judge Learned Hand. "It is the business of the soul to impose her own order upon the clamorous rout; to establish a hierarchy appropriate to the demands of her own nature, and by the mere fiat of her absolute choice, if that be based upon self-knowledge." [15] The Soviet Idea has a comparatively primitive conception of man as a being who can be almost infinitely manipulated. The love and friendship of people for each other are precluded; affection and loyalty are directed toward an impersonal State and its creations. The State must be valued more than friend or family. This overtone was nicely expressed by a young Soviet writer who had been tried for his views but part of whose diary the State apparently felt it must publish.

> To love people means that when you meet a person and talk with that person, you know how to place yourself in his position, you know how to live with his thoughts and with his sorrows, and you know how to forgive him that which you would forgive yourself and help him the way you would help your-

self, i.e., without charity, naturally, with all your strength, as if it were for your own sake.[16]

When we speak of spreading the American Idea, we want to be very clear at the outset that we are *not* talking simply about the "American way of life" or the "American way of doing things" but, rather, the idea we have described in terms of its basic assumptions—an Idea which can guide diverse people in diverse ways according to their own unique cultural backgrounds and their own resources.

The Soviet political system which was developed to spread the Soviet Idea has some apparent operational advantages over the political system developed to embody the American Idea. The Soviets have a highly trained and a highly dedicated leadership not subject to required periodic change; they are able to coordinate guidance and manipulation through a highly centralized and systematic educational program at all levels and to adjust their economy to suit their purposes, including favorable trade arrangements to other nations

95

as it suits their international strategy. The tight internal Party organization means there will be no compromising with minority parties and that once decisions are made, they can be quickly carried out. With Moscow as the center of world Communism and most Communist states currently following their lead, with notable exceptions, there can be long-range planning and efficient cooperation. All Communist countries, for example, can be directed to support Castro in Cuba and loyal Party members in nearly every part of the world can be trained to foment riots or revolutions when the signal is given.

By contrast the American Idea faces certain dilemmas inherent in its democratic political system. I refer here only to a few of these dilemmas which a wise American, Chester Barnard, has pointed out. One he calls "the dilemma of consent and conformance," the democratic method being "one of decision by partial consent, whereas cooperative action requires substantially complete conformance." Another he labels "the dilemma of the abstract and the concrete" by which he refers to the discrepancy "between the verbalization of ideas and the specific activities to which they refer." A third is the dilemma of "time lag" to describe the long intervals that elapse "between the need for action and decision; and between decision and corresponding execution." Still another is "the dilemma of political conflict" which "often requires weak compromises or results in failure to make some decisions urgently needed." And, finally, we may cite what Barnard calls "the dilemma of effective action and politics" because the choice to be made by democratic leaders "usually requires some modification of the ideal aim to one adapted to the capacities, emotions, and wills of the individuals whose efforts must accomplish it; and simultaneously some modification of the latter by training, precept, example, and inspiration." [17]

In spite of these dilemmas, the American Idea seems to work and to hold the possibility for people to create continually a kind of environment that better enables them to carry out their purposes. It seems to correspond to the basic characteristics of man as well as any political idea yet devised. Certainly one reason for its success is its self-conscious emphasis on change, its guarantee of the right to protest, its self-alteration, its ever-becomingness. Within the American Idea there can be nothing static about the pursuit of happiness: It is a process involving movement, novelty, adventure, trying new things in new ways, trying to figure out what will work as new problems arise. It involves testing the products of thought to see if the consequences they intend will actually come true in experience. American pragmatism with its notion that truth must be validated in terms of what works is no accident; the pragmatic question "does it work?" is answered by the pragmatic question "is it successful in achieving the intended purpose?"

Nor is the American Idea something for America alone. It has traveled on its own and has shown itself to be self-propelling. The American Idea is something people everywhere can understand. It expresses the longings of all people and can be readily translated into local terms. We are told by those who closely followed events in the Hungarian Revolution that the last broadcast heard by the outside world from the Budapest radio before the rebellion was finally crushed by Soviet force was a reading of Lincoln's Gettysburg Address, containing as it does the famous phrase so like the original description of the American Idea by Theodore Parker. Again, I refer to Carl Sandburg who has expressed the point so well.

> You may sell an idea to the people
> And sit back satisfied you have them your way
> But will they stay sold on the idea?
> Will they be easy to hold in line
> Unless the idea has a promise of roots
> Twisted deep in the heart of man
> Being brought into play. . . .[18]

But if the American Idea is to be given a fair chance to be translated into local terms, certain conditions must be fostered or maintained. As a Communist writer has pointed out, "The most ferocious ideological struggle between two systems, between two world outlooks, between two conceptions of the future of mankind, has been, is being, and will be waged in the world." [19]

Here are a few of the conditions that would seem to be psychologically important if the conflict is to be won and won peacefully.

Obviously, we must keep ourselves strong as a nation so that there will never be a doubt that the center of the American Idea means to preserve itself, come what may. Obviously, too, we should

99

help people understand some of the discrepancies in the Soviet Idea between reality as experienced and reality as pictured: showing people in uncommitted areas how the Communist Party uses nations and states and the people who compose them as instruments or tools to carry out Party policies; making clear to people that the issue dividing the world is not "Communism" versus "Capitalism" but the dictatorship of the Communist Party versus the possibility of national development in a free and open way; illustrating that while Soviet leaders talk about "coexistence," in reality they seem to be afraid of it, continually insulating their people from outside news and information while imposing restrictions on travel.

But our effort must, above all, be positive. We must keep our own shortcomings clearly visible to ourselves and remedy them as quickly as possible, acknowledging our blunders and mistakes, to demonstrate to people everywhere that the American Idea is self-correcting with continued and never-ending frontiers that have no boundaries and that present an endless challenge. Tagore once wrote, "A lamp can never light another lamp unless it continues to burn its own flame." By extending our frontiers to a concern for people in other nations, Americans themselves can experience the zest that comes from coping with and overcoming the undetermined as we aid others in their pursuit of happiness.

A fundamental problem is to help people lift themselves to a level where primitive appeals which lead only to their own enslavement no longer suffice. The Soviet Idea is bound to wither away if democracies are quick enough to help people become politically sophisticated by assisting them to raise their standards of living step by step and in their own terms, by aiding them to better health, by speeding their literacy and education, and by satisfying all the other requirements for personal and political development.

To accomplish these things will require constant updating of American methods and solutions in terms of the new conditions created. Even such great documents as the Ten Commandments and the Declaration of Independence are inadequate in furnishing guides to some of the problems we must recognize and resolve today and which were completely undreamt of in earlier times. Especially baffling in this age of specialists and mutual dependence is the fact that many things are happening to many people who at the same time are not themselves actively participating in bringing about the events that engulf them. The result is that most people have no clear understanding of the basic factors that have created the problems they face. And if they do get a glimmering of why the problem exists, they so often feel its resolution is almost completely outside their bailiwick. As a glaring example, it is doubtful that more than 1/100th of one per cent of educated Westerners, if even that many, really know how a missile armed with an atomic warhead is made and what damage it can actually do. And only a tiny handful of men will be involved in the decision as to whether or not such a weapon will ever be used. It is small wonder that socially minded scientists feel a most pressing obligation to try to convey to laymen some of the information that is so much a part of their own daily thinking and that holds such a fateful bearing on human destiny.

In the competition of ideologies to show people what possibilities are available and what they can want, the American Idea clearly has the widest range of offerings of the highest quality. For it can display a whole array of experiences available *after* security and stability are attained. On the other hand, any political system that denies freedom does violence to the human design. As we help people raise their standards of living, of health, and of education we must at the same time be quite clear in our own minds and make it quite clear to them that no increase in these standards alone will ever reconcile human beings to a permanent condition of unfreedom which denies the possibility of achieving so many of the most characteristic value-satisfactions men are capable of.

Americans must find out from people in other countries *in their own terms* what they are, what they are trying to do, what they are trying to become. This can never be done if the primary concern of Americans is to tell other people what they should be doing in order to be more like us. Such a simple, common-sense precept is often forgotten in American information and aid programs as well as in statements concerning the objectives of organized American efforts like the Peace Corps.

We must treat people in other nations not only the way they are now but the way they want to become and to be. Like the flower girl, Liza, in

Shaw's *Pygmalion,* who felt like a lady when she was treated like a lady, the way a nation is treated by others can to a large extent determine that nation's image of itself. "To be accepted and to be treasured are indications if not final proofs that a government is a success."[20] In writing of the community in which she lived, Louise Rich observed, "It is an interesting fact that usually the people whom you start being decent to on principle, you end by liking in practice."[21] So it is and can be in the relationship between nations no matter what their cultural diversity may be.

And this means, of course, that we must respect not only the national independence of new nations but also the desire so many of them have to be neutral in whatever ideological battles go on around them—a deep desire also shared by more advanced nations like Japan for independence, neutrality, and a self-respect based on world respect. We should not forget that for over a hundred years our own foreign policy was guided by Washington's Farewell Address in which he expressed similar desires for the new nation he had led into being: "With me a predominant motive has been to endeavor to gain time to our country to settle and mature its yet recent institutions, and to progress without interruption to that degree of strength and consistency which is necessary to give it, humanly speaking, the command of its own fortunes." Furthermore, America must try to become self-conscious of the fact that "neutrality" itself is a relative term, that what appears as "neutral" behavior to the people of one nation may appear—because of its very neutrality—highly partisan behavior to the people of another nation. For example, what the United States State Department may regard as a "neutral" policy with respect to Israel will likely be regarded by Nasser as a pro-Israel policy since from his point of view the very existence of Israel should not be acknowledged.

Two experiences I have had during the past few years illustrate some of the basic problems underlying the accommodation of political systems to human nature. In one of the colleges I visited in India a tea was given for me by the 150 faculty members. As guest of honor, I was shuttled by the president of the college from one table to another where I met different faculty groups. While sitting with one group, we somehow began to discuss the nature of reality. After a few minutes I was taken from this group and moved to another. At the end of the tea, when the president of the college was hurrying me off to another building some blocks away where I was to lecture, I happened to pass the little group of professors with whom I had been discussing the nature of reality. I quipped to them as I walked down the driveway, "Have you figured out yet what is real?" One of them, quick as a flash, extended his hand to me and said, "A handshake." We shook hands and I was whisked off. It is relevant to mention here that I had been told this particular professor, a very fine fellow indeed, was one of the leading Communist intellectuals in India.

In 1958, I visited the Soviet Union with two other psychologists and two experienced observers of the Soviet Union. Our arrival at Moscow was delayed two days because of weather and our own change of the air route by means of which we were to come. As we got off the plane, our Intourist guide introduced himself. We said we hoped our delay had not inconvenienced him. He replied sharply, "It did." After we had driven from the airport to the hotel, I wanted to make sure our guide knew all the members of our party since in the rush of clearing at the airport I was not sure all of us knew who was who. In introducing him I casually referred to him as "our friend," and he quickly replied, "Better not call me a friend until you know me. Wait and we'll see later if we are friends." It appeared as though he had been indoctrinated in arrogance and contempt.

But the story continues.

He proved to be an excellent interpreter, sometimes having to handle rather difficult concepts as we lectured at the universities and as he translated during technical sessions with our Soviet colleagues. He also proved to be extremely efficient in arranging our transportation and appointments, seeing that our luggage got to the right places, etc. He was with us constantly, eating at the same table whenever we were outside of Moscow. He witnessed our joking and banter, our American freedom to talk and to wander about separately or in pairs if we wanted to. He was with us at the official banquets when we toasted our Soviet colleagues and they toasted us. He saw the mutual respect academic colleagues had for each other. We Americans toasted him for his able help. Toward the end of our visit he even joined in the convivial conversation by offering a few jokes of his own.

As we left the hotel to ride out to the airport, I was alone with this loyal and patriotic young man for a moment and thanked him genuinely for his help. His eyes moistened and he asked us to be sure to send him some of the books we had written. At the airport itself, in bidding us good-bye, he could not hide his tears. Just what was going on in his mind one can only guess.

Notes

Chapter 1. Some Political Consequences of Being Human

1. Fëdor Dostoevski, *Letters from the Underworld,* translated with an introduction by C. J. Hogarth (Everyman's Library, London: J. M. Dent & Sons, Ltd.; New York: E. P. Dutton & Co., Inc., 1957), pp. 25, 39, 40.
2. Sir Russell Brain, *Mind, Perception and Science* (Oxford: Blackwell Scientific Publications, 1951), pp. 43–46.
3. Dostoevski, *op. cit.,* p. 37.
4. Martin Buber, *I and Thou* (Edinburgh: T. & T. Clark; New York: Charles Scribner's Sons, 1937), p. 27.
5. Max Frankel, *New York Times,* November 27, 1960, p. 35.
6. Niccolo Tucci, "The Underground Letters," *The New Yorker,* August 4, 1951, p. 24.
7. Tad Szulc, "Castro Tries to Export 'Fidelismo'," *New York Times Magazine,* November 27, 1960, pp. 19ff.
8. F. J. Turner, *Frontier in American History* (New York: Henry Holt and Company, 1920), p. 293.
9. C. L. Sulzberger, *New York Times,* February 25, 1959.

Notes

Chapter 2. The Quality of Political Awareness

1. G. Lowes Dickinson, *The Greek View of Life* (New York: Doubleday, Doran & Co., 1931), p. 72.
2. Albert Camus, *The Rebel* (New York: Vintage Books, 1960), p. 304.
3. Joseph Alsop, "The History Maker," *Herald Tribune* (New York), December 2, 1958.
4. Aldous Huxley, *Brave New World Revisited* (New York: Harper and Brothers, 1958), pp. 38f.
5. Bernard Kalb, "Jakarta: The Sukarno Orbit," *New York Times Magazine*, October 29, 1960, p. 15.
6. Milton Meltzer, *Mark Twain Himself* (New York: Thomas Y. Crowell Co., 1960), p. 260.
7. Carl Van Doren, *Benjamin Franklin.* (New York: Viking Press, 1938), p. 329.
8. Tom Mboya, "Key Questions for Awakening Africa," *New York Times Magazine,* June 28, 1959, p. 39.
9. Van Doren, *op. cit.*, p. 484.
10. Henry Steele Commager, *The American Mind* (New Haven: Yale University Press, 1950), p. 22.
11. John Macmurray, *The Self as Agent* (London: Faber & Faber, Ltd., 1957), p. 30.
12. Stuart Chase, *Some Things Worth Knowing* (New York: Harper and Brothers, 1958), pp. 208f.
13. Jacques Maritain, *Three Reformers* (London: Sheed & Ward, 1928), p. 14.
14. A. M. Rosenthal, *New York Times*, October 17, 1960, p. 8.
15. Learned Hand, *The Bill of Rights* (Cambridge, Mass.: Harvard University Press, 1958), pp. 75f.
16. Camus, *op. cit.*, p. 78.
17. Huxley, *op. cit.*, p. 56.
18. *The Indian Social Reformer,* February 1, 1952.
19. Osgood Caruthers, "Nasser, the Nile and the Fellah," *New York Times Magazine,* October 21, 1956.
20. Sir Julian Huxley, "Cultural Process and Evolution," in

Behavior and Evolution, edited by Anne Roe and George Gaylord Simpson (New Haven: Yale University Press, 1958), pp. 437ff.

21. Edward C. Banfield, *The Moral Basis of a Backward Society* (Glencoe, Ill.: The Free Press, 1958), p. 85.
22. Daniel Lerner and David Riesman, "Self and Society: Reflections on Some Turks in Transition," *Explorations,* June 1955, No. 5, pp. 68–80.
23. For an insightful discussion of this point, see George Gerbner, "The Individual in a Mass Culture," *Saturday Review,* June 18, 1960, pp. 11ff.
24. Lloyd A. Free, *A Brief Report on the Dynamics of Philippine Politics* (Princeton, N. J.: Institute for International Social Research, April, 1960).
25. Paul Grimes, "In Pakistan: 'Maybe He Can Help Us'," *New York Times Magazine,* November 27, 1960, p. 116.

Chapter 3. Pressures and Possibilities

1. From *Good Morning, America,* copyright, 1928, 1956, by Carl Sandburg, p. 20f. Reprinted by permission of Harcourt, Brace & World, Inc.
2. From *The People, Yes,* by Carl Sandburg, p. 134, copyright, 1936, by Harcourt, Brace & World, Inc.
3. Lucian W. Pye, *The Policy Implications of Social Change in Non-Western Societies* (Cambridge, Mass.: Massachusetts Institute of Technology, Center for International Studies, 1957), pp. 10ff.
4. Richard L. Walker, "Chairman Mao and the Cult of Personality," *Encounter,* Vol. 14, No. 6 (June 1960), p. 42.
5. *Ibid.,* p. 38.
6. Julius K. Nyerere, "Africa Needs Time," *New York Times Magazine,* March 27, 1960, p. 84.
7. Text of a Statement Issued by the Conference of Representatives of Communist Parties, *New York Times,* December 7, 1960, p. 14.

Notes

8. C. P. Snow. *Science and Government*. (Cambridge, Mass.: Harvard University Press, 1960), p. 80.
9. Horace Kallen, *Cultural Pluralism and the American Idea* (Philadelphia: University of Pennsylvania Press, 1956), p. 61.
10. Hadley Cantril, *Soviet Leaders and Mastery Over Man* (New Brunswick, N.J.: Rutgers University Press, 1960), p. vii f.
11. B. P. Yesipov and N. K. Goncharov, "Developing Conscious Discipline," *Pedagogika* (5th ed.; Moscow: Uchpedgiz, 1950), ch. 15.
12. Text of a Statement Issued by the Conference of Representatives of Communist Parties, *op. cit.*, p. 15.
13. Robert Tucker, *Philosophy and Myth in Karl Marx* (New York: Cambridge University Press, 1961).
14. V. I. Lenin, *Collected Works* (1st ed.; Moscow, 1923), Vol. XVII, p. 145.
15. Learned Hand, *The Spirit of Liberty* (New York: Alfred A. Knopf, Inc., 1952), p. 113.
16. Victor Golovinsky, *Komsomolskaya Pravda*, March 29, 1959 (Translated by Vera Dunham).
17. Chester Barnard, *Organization and Management* (Cambridge, Mass.: Harvard University Press, 1948), pp. 30–45.
18. Carl Sandburg, *The People, Yes, op. cit.*, 185f.
19. Konstantin Simonov, "Drama, Theatre, and Life," *Sovietskoi Iskusstvo*, November 23, 1948.
20. D. W. Brogan, *America in the Modern World* (New Brunswick, N.J.: Rutgers University Press, 1960), p. 26.
21. Louise Dickinson Rich, *My Neck of the Woods* (Philadelphia: J. B. Lippincott Company, 1950), p. 207.